Georgia O'Keeffe

Robyn Montana Turner

Little, Brown and Company

Boston   Toronto   London

This book is dedicated
to my daughter, Tara,
who holds Georgia O'Keeffe
as a role model.

ACKNOWLEDGMENTS
   I'd like to extend my grateful appreciation to the many individuals who influenced
the development of this series and this book, including: Maria Modugno and her
assistant editor, Hilary M. Breed, for tenaciously seeing this book through to
completion; Virginia A. Creeden for gathering permissions for the images from around
the world; Judy Lopez and the Estate of Georgia O'Keeffe for their helpful assistance;
Dr. Emilio Caballero, Art Professor Emeritus of West Texas State University, for
relating information about O'Keeffe's tenure there and for teaching me about the art
and aesthetics of O'Keeffe's spiritual home, the plains; my mother and daughter for
reviewing the manuscript and providing insight; my father, son, other family members,
and friends for their encouragement; other biographers of women artists; and the many
museums and collectors whose photographs appear in the series.

First Edition

Library of Congress Cataloging-in-Publication Data

Turner, Robyn.
   Georgia O'Keeffe / by Robyn Montana Turner. — 1st ed.
      p. cm. — (Portraits of women artists for children)
   Summary: A biography of a prominent American artist renowned for
   her images of gigantic flowers, cityscapes, and distinctive desert
   scenes.
   ISBN 0-316-856495-7
   1. O'Keeffe, Georgia, 1887–1986 — Juvenile literature.
   2. Painters — United States — Biography — Juvenile literature.
   [1. O'Keeffe, Georgia, 1887–1986. 2. Artists.] I. Title.
   II. Series.
   ND237.05T87   1991
   759.13 — dc20
   [B]
   [92]   90-19352

10 9 8 7 6 5 4 3 2 1

TWP

Published simultaneously in Canada
by Little, Brown & Company (Canada) Limited

Printed in Singapore

I found I could say things with color
and shapes that I couldn't say in any
other way — things I had no words for.

— Georgia O'Keeffe

4

4

Georgia O'Keeffe
1887–1986

Just 150 years ago, only a few women in the world had become well known as artists. Since then many women have been recognized for their artwork. Today some very famous artists are women.

Nowadays both boys and girls are encouraged to become great artists by attending art schools where they study together with the finest art teachers. Both men and women learn to draw, paint, and sculpt images of the human body by studying nude models.

But let's imagine that you could go back in time to the turn of the twentieth century — about a hundred years ago. As a young person growing up in America then, you might wonder why women artists in your country have just recently been allowed to attend the best schools of art. You might question why women artists are not welcome at social gatherings where male artists learn from each other by discussing new ideas about art. You might be surprised to discover that women have just recently been permitted to look at nude models to help them learn how to portray the human figure. And you might be disappointed to learn that most young girls are not encouraged to become great artists.

During that time, about a century ago in America, there lived a young girl who later became well known as an artist. Her name was Georgia O'Keeffe. Today her works of art hang in museums throughout the world.

Alfred Stieglitz. **Georgia O'Keeffe.** *1918. Photograph. The Metropolitan Museum of Art, Gift of David A. Schulte, 1928 (28.127.1). All rights reserved. The Metropolitan Museum of Art.*

O'Keeffe Farmhouse. *The State Historical Society of Wisconsin.*

On November 15, 1887, a baby girl named Georgia Totto O'Keeffe was born to Ida and Francis O'Keeffe in their farmhouse near Sun Prairie, Wisconsin. The dark-haired infant was named for her mother's Hungarian father, George Totto. She was the second of seven O'Keeffe children.

Even as a child, Georgia showed signs of becoming an artist. Colors and patterns stood out to her. One day, before she was even a year old, she was carried outside and placed on a quilt. Many years later she recalled the bright sunshine and the patterns on the quilt — red and white flowers and tiny red stars. And she had a vivid imagination. While her sisters and brothers played games inside the cool dairy barn, she would gather up her small china dolls for an afternoon of pretending beneath the hemlock and apple trees.

At other times Georgia enjoyed the company of others. Both grandmothers — strong frontier women — shared Georgia's creative spirit. They both dabbled in art, and Grandmother O'Keeffe's paintings of fruit and moss rose hung in the farmhouse. Georgia loved to be with her father, who kept his pockets filled with sweets and played the Irish fiddle. They liked to walk together through the fields to check the growth of cornstalks and to discover signs of nature's changing seasons. Georgia preferred her father's love of the land to her mother's love of books. But the young girl's imagination soared each night as Ida read aloud to her tales of adventure that took place in the Wild West of Texas and New Mexico.

Two months before her fifth birthday, Georgia started school in the same one-room schoolhouse her parents had attended many years before. But Ida felt her daughter needed more training in art than the small school offered.

In 1893 Georgia's mother never imagined it would be possible for her young daughter to become a painter of fine works of art that would hang in museums throughout the world. In those days women's art — baskets, quilts, pottery, decorative drawings and paintings — was not considered important enough to be exhibited in art museums. Ida wanted all of her daughters to learn to paint decorative items, which she thought would help them become proper "ladies" in society. She hoped they might even become art teachers, too.

When Georgia was twelve, Ida arranged for her daughters to begin their training by taking private drawing and painting lessons. Each Saturday they traveled seven miles round-trip by horse and buggy. The girls were taught to copy pictures from a stack of prints the teacher kept in a cupboard. In these classes, Georgia discovered that she liked to paint with watercolors. When she got home she sometimes

Caricatures of Teachers.
"The Mortar Board." 1905.
*Courtesy of Chatham Hall,
Chatham, Virginia.*
At fifteen, Georgia
sometimes drew with a sense
of humor. She had fun
creating these caricatures of
her teachers at Chatham.

painted an imaginary scene of her own — such as palm trees waving in the ocean breeze near a lighthouse. Georgia had her own ideas about how her artwork should look. She hated it when her teacher touched up her paintings.

One day that year, Georgia blurted out to her friend Lena, "I am going to be an artist!" — her new lifetime goal. Georgia never knew exactly why she decided to become an artist. After all, her schoolbooks had never mentioned any women artists. She had never met a professional artist. Her only inspiration had been a small pen-and-ink drawing of a Grecian maiden in one of her mother's books. Georgia wanted to create something as beautiful as that drawing.

A few years later, in 1902, the O'Keeffe family became restless with farm life and left Wisconsin to begin anew in Williamsburg, Virginia. In time, Ida — still intent upon making a lady of her daughter — enrolled Georgia in a boarding school for girls in Chatham, Virginia.

Georgia's high-school classmates at Chatham Episcopal Institute liked her because, at age fifteen, she was different, mischievous, artistic, and fun. Whereas they wore tightly fitted dresses with ruffles and bows, Georgia designed and sewed her own clothes to appear tailored and plain. She wore her hair pulled back and held by a ribbon at the bottom of a braid.

In the art studio at Chatham, Georgia painted at an easel in the center of the room. For hours at a time she remained perfectly silent and unaware of the chatter around her. But occasionally she would feel a burst of energy and create a commotion by making her classmates laugh.

She sketched caricatures of the teachers and sometimes got into trouble for going for walks or staying awake too late. But her art teacher encouraged her. The girls chose Georgia to be the art editor of the school's first yearbook. And Georgia's watercolor painting of red and yellow corn won the Chatham art prize.

After graduating from Chatham, Georgia went to Chicago to study at the Art Institute there. Since the turn of the century, female students had been admitted to most American art schools. But even so, in 1905, Ida was considered ahead of her time for sending her daughter to a school where students studied nude models.

During the first day of anatomy class at the Art Institute, students drew pictures of a male model who wore only a loincloth. Georgia was embarrassed, even though she had never thought anything about swimming in the river with a boy her age who wore, as she put it, "the least little piece of a bathing suit." Soon she became accustomed to drawing images of nude models, but she never developed a strong interest in portraying the human figure.

In 1907, after recovering from typhoid fever, Georgia moved to New York City. There she became a member of the Art Students League, a popular art school, where one of her paintings won top prize. From her teacher William Merritt Chase, she learned how to use white paint to brighten her pictures. He taught her how to paint still lifes of brass and copper pots and pans, peppers, onions, and other objects. She painted them so well it appeared she had used only one grand brushstroke.

Georgia O'Keeffe, yearbook photograph. "The Mortar Board." 1905. *Courtesy of Chatham Hall, Chatham, Virginia.*

One snowy day a classmate suggested they all go to "291" to see an exhibit of the much-talked-about drawings of Auguste Rodin, a French artist. Georgia knew that 291 was the Fifth Avenue gallery of the well-known photographer Alfred Stieglitz (STEE glits), a powerful leader in the art world.

Georgia was not impressed that day with the new style of artwork from France. It appeared to her as only curved lines and scratches. Neither was she especially taken with Alfred Stieglitz, who glared at the students from behind his pince-nez eyeglasses — "pinched" to his nose by a spring. Toward the end of her life, however, she would marvel at the same Rodin drawings. And within only a few years, Georgia O'Keeffe and Alfred Stieglitz would discover a mutual admiration.

During her early twenties Georgia reluctantly put away her canvases and brushes to take a job as a commercial illustrator in Chicago, where she drew advertisements. She could no longer afford to go to art school, and women were discouraged at that time from striving to become serious artists. Soon her family back in Virginia suffered health and financial problems. Sadly, Georgia decided she must give up her dream of becoming an artist. To add to her problems, a terrible bout with measles temporarily affected her eyesight. So at twenty-three, Georgia moved back to Virginia.

When she recovered, her sisters persuaded her to enroll in an art class at the nearby University of Virginia. And there, Alon Bement, her new art teacher, rekindled her creative energy.

Bement talked about some of the new ideas he had learned in New York from his teacher, Arthur Wesley Dow. Georgia was fascinated with Dow's belief that filling space in a beautiful way gives even simple tasks — such as addressing a letter, combing your hair, or choosing your shoes — an artful quality. She also liked Dow's new way of composing a picture by dividing a square into geometric shapes such as circles and triangles. Georgia set aside her realistic paintings — those that looked familiar and ordinary to the viewer — and began to experiment with this notion of abstract art. From Dow's theories, she gathered an artistic "alphabet" — tools for creating her own style.

Tent Door at Night shows Georgia's new approach to art. With watercolor she painted two large curving triangles — the flaps of a pup tent as seen from the inside. Other triangular shapes represent the sky and the tent floor. The tent's pole divides the space into yet more triangles. In this somewhat abstract painting, Georgia practiced filling the space with harmony and beauty.

Georgia O'Keeffe. **Tent Door at Night.** *c. 1913. Watercolor on paper. University of New Mexico Art Museum; purchase through the Julius Rolshoven Memorial Fund, with the assistance of the Friends of Art (72.157).* Georgia tried out the ideas of Professor Arthur Wesley Dow by painting this rectangle with triangles in the middle. She divided the space with curved and straight lines.

Georgia O'Keeffe. **Drawing XIII.** *1915. Charcoal on paper. 24½ × 19 inches. The Metropolitan Museum of Art. The Alfred Stieglitz Collection, 1950 (50.236.2). Photograph by Malcolm Varon.*
By working with only sticks of charcoal and paper, Georgia got in touch with her innermost thoughts and feelings.

In 1914 Georgia gathered together the savings she had earned from four summers of assisting Bement and from teaching art in the public schools of faraway Amarillo, Texas. Determined once again to become an artist, she made her way to New York City to study with Professor Arthur Wesley Dow.

In Dow's classes at Columbia University, Georgia's brushes were always the best and her colors the brightest. Georgia and another student, Anita Pollitzer, often rode the trolley together to Stieglitz's gallery at 291 Fifth Avenue to examine the newest American and European art.

In 1915, in order to support herself, Georgia accepted a teaching position — this time at a women's college in South Carolina. Alone during her off-hours, she hung all of her paintings on the wall of her studio, sat down, and studied them. Georgia realized she had yet to find her own style. Each painting had been done to please a teacher or to resemble the style of a well-known artist.

So she put away all of her paintings, her watercolor and oil paints, and her brushes. At twenty-seven, Georgia decided to begin again. She took out her black charcoal and stacks of blank paper. Suddenly there was so much to say that she felt the whole side of a wall would not be large enough to contain it. It was as if her mind had created shapes she knew nothing about. Night after night she sat on the floor drawing images that were hers alone. As her ideas and feelings gushed onto the paper, Georgia worried that she could be losing her mind.

At last the frenzy was over. She began to realize that, as an educated artist, she must now feel free to go beyond the rules she had been taught. Soon the "new artist" wanted to show her creations to someone else. She packed up some of her drawings

and sent them to Anita in New York. Georgia's only instructions were for her friend not to show the drawings to anybody.

But Anita became so excited about Georgia's charcoal drawings that she disregarded her friend's instructions and showed the drawings to Stieglitz. He expressed his joy in the discovery of "the purest, finest, sincerest things that have entered 291 in a long while."

During the spring of 1916, Georgia accepted an offer to return the next fall to the Texas Panhandle, this time to teach art at West Texas State Normal College. With only a few months to prepare, she moved to New York City to study once again with Professor Arthur Wesley Dow. One day she learned that without her permission, Stieglitz was exhibiting the drawings Anita had shown him. Georgia stormed into 291 and demanded an explanation. Stieglitz explained that her drawings were so wonderful he simply had to exhibit them. Following a heated argument, Georgia silently decided that the advantages of having her drawings exhibited at 291 outweighed the issue at hand. The two artists then had lunch together.

Georgia could hardly wait to venture once again into the Wild West that she had imagined as a child. Since the day two years ago when her train had chugged into the depot of the flat and wide-open spaces of Amarillo, Georgia had been inspired by the Texas landscape. The wind gusted constantly. Tumbleweeds and dust raced across the plains. Covered with dust, Georgia sometimes did not recognize herself in the mirror except for the shape of her clothes. For the rest of her life she would speak of the plains — "the terrible winds and a wonderful emptiness" — as her spiritual home.

West Texas State Normal College. *Courtesy of the Panhandle-Plains Historical Museum, Canyon, Texas.* Georgia taught art at West Texas State Normal College.

In September Georgia settled down in Canyon, Texas, a small college town near the rim of the rugged and colorful Palo Duro Canyon, which looks like a smaller version of the Grand Canyon. During her year there, Georgia loved to walk away from Canyon onto the plains at dusk. Only the evening star shone through the colors of the setting sun.

Evening Star III represents her fascination with that lone star as the setting sun beamed beneath it. She painted ten versions of the evening star in watercolor. Now that Georgia had her own style, she could express her feelings about nature in an abstract way.

Georgia O'Keeffe. **Evening Star, III.** *1917. Watercolor on paper. 9 × 11⅞ inches. Collection, The Museum of Modern Art, New York. Mr. and Mrs. Donald B. Straus Fund.*
Georgia loved to find the first star at sunset. Through color and line she expressed what it meant to her.

15

During Georgia's three semesters at West Texas State, she and Alfred Stieglitz kept in touch. Through letters and brief visits, they fell in love. He liked her paintings, and she liked his photographs. They were interested in each other's creativity. In 1918 Georgia accepted Stieglitz's offer to leave Texas and join him in New York. After several years together in New York, on December 11, 1924, they were married. Georgia chose to keep her own last name.

In 1925 they moved into an apartment on the highest floor of one of New York's modern skyscrapers, the Shelton. During the cold winter months, the howling wind shook the huge steel frame until the couple felt as if they were adrift in the middle of an ocean.

Georgia created *The Shelton with Sunspots* by starting in the upper left corner of the canvas and painting to the lower right corner without retracing her steps. In this view, looking up at the Shelton from the sidewalk, she even captured on canvas the sun's "bite" out of one side of the skyscraper. Georgia created patterns of small sunspots and wavy lines — as though her eyes were playing tricks on her after having looked at the hot sunburst.

Georgia O'Keeffe. **The Shelton with Sunspots.** *1926. Oil on canvas. 123.2 × 76.8 cm. Gift of Leigh B. Block (1985.206). © 1990 The Art Institute of Chicago, All Rights Reserved. Photography courtesy of The Art Institute of Chicago.* Georgia looked up at the Shelton, and the sun shone in her eyes. She decided to capture those sunspots on canvas.

Alfred Stieglitz (1864–
1946). **Georgia O'Keeffe:
A Portrait.** *1918. Gelatin
silver photograph. 3½ ×
4½ inches. National
Gallery of Art, Washington,
Alfred Stieglitz Collection
(D–1409).*
At Lake George, Georgia
rested and painted. She
created images of tiny
flowers and other natural
subjects.

For many years O'Keeffe and Stieglitz enjoyed summers at his family's summer home at Lake George in upstate New York. Georgia especially liked being alone or with only Stieglitz by her side — away from people who disturbed her concentration and, she said, made her feel "like a hobbled horse." In the country her free spirit renewed itself. She picked wild strawberries, hunted for watercress, gardened, dozed, read, swam, and hiked the hills.

Rested, Georgia set about to paint images of the Lake George area — tiny flowers, shells, leaves, sweeping landscapes, barns, and windows. Her style for many of these paintings was realistic. But some of her most abstract works also were painted at Lake George. In those she made shape, form, and color create only the idea of the real subject and the way she felt about it. To her surprise, many of her paintings that she thought looked like the real subject appeared abstract to some viewers.

Her abstract painting *From the Lake No. 1* shows sharp, curving, and swollen forms seeming to create the stormy rhythm of Lake George. In the foreground Georgia painted tints and shades of greens and blues — cool colors — perhaps to suggest the turbulent water below. In the background, on the top part of the canvas, shades of gray look like steam rising from the water.

Whether she was at Lake George or in her Manhattan studio, Georgia used a tray made of glass for mixing her paints. On this palette she kept a separate brush for each color so as not to muddy any of them. She put a sample of each color onto its own white card so that she could reproduce the exact shade or tint for another painting. Art critics praised Georgia's technical abilities. Many of the male artists in Stieglitz's circle, however, thought her colors were too bright.

Georgia O'Keeffe. **From the Lake No. 1.** *1924. Oil on canvas. 37⅛ × 31 inches. Purchased with funds from the Coffin Fine Arts Trust, Nathan Emory Coffin Collection of the Des Moines Art Center.*

This abstract painting shows how Georgia felt about Lake George. Her broad brushstrokes and cool color selections suggest that she sensed a special energy within the lake.

In 1925 Georgia became annoyed with a critic for referring to her as a "woman painter" rather than as simply a "painter." She knew that women in those days were not considered the best artists. Even so, the critic added that Georgia "outblazes the other painters."

Perhaps the critic had seen *Red Canna*, in which Georgia's reds, oranges, and yellows — warm colors — indeed outblaze almost any painting. With her palette of oil paints she created a close-up view of the tropical flower, making it appear to explode off the edges of the canvas. Warm and shiny colors radiate from the center. The ruffled petal forms create a rhythm that ripples and flows.

Throughout her lifetime Georgia painted hundreds of flower images of every color, shape, form, and variety. She tried with her paintings to make even the busy New Yorkers notice the beauty of these flowers. Cleverly, Georgia increased the scale, or size, of her flower paintings to fill big canvases and appear much larger than the real flowers. When people asked her why she made her flowers so large, she asked them why they never wondered why she made her rivers so small. Georgia expressed on canvas what she saw in her mind and felt in her heart. And all of New York took notice.

Georgia O'Keeffe. **Red Canna.** *c. 1924. Oil on canvas mounted on masonite. 36 × 29⅞ inches (91.4 × 76.0 cm.). Collection of The University of Arizona Museum of Art, Gift of Oliver James.*
For this painting, Georgia expressed herself with a palette of warm colors — reds, oranges, and yellows. At other times she chose cool colors — blues, greens, and violets.

Poppies were one of Georgia's favorite subjects. *Oriental Poppies* shows two blossoms filling the canvas in symmetrical balance. To achieve symmetry, Georgia positioned the flowers evenly so that if the canvas were folded in half, each side would appear about the same. Her palette of warm colors for *Oriental Poppies* was like that of *Red Canna*. However, the centers of the poppies — velvety dark shades — are contrasted against the light tints of the edges of the petals. In this way the viewer's eye is drawn deep into the core of the blossoms.

Like the dark and mysterious focal points of Georgia's poppies, the two well-known Manhattan artists — O'Keeffe and Stieglitz — almost always wore black clothing. Stieglitz sported a dramatic black cape. Georgia often wore a white silk blouse covered by a black wool coat with a collar that buttoned up to her chin. Her gloves were made of fine black leather. His untamed white hair complemented her sleek black knot drawn back to the nape of her neck.

Georgia loved to sew her own clothes because it gave her time to think freely and solve problems. Black outfits helped her feel unnoticeable, and they let others know she preferred to be taken seriously.

Georgia O'Keeffe. **Oriental Poppies.** *1928. Oil on canvas. 30 × 40⅛ inches. Collection University Art Museum, University of Minnesota, Minneapolis (Purchase).*

Sometimes Georgia filled the whole canvas with one subject. In *Oriental Poppies,* she showed how two subjects can work together to achieve symmetrical balance.

By 1929 Georgia wanted to see new country. Stieglitz decided not to go with her, but he realized that Georgia had to travel to satisfy her artistic appetite. Her pioneering spirit inspired her to go west to New Mexico to visit artist friends she had met in New York.

When Georgia arrived in New Mexico, she knew it was hers. She spent the summer in Taos, an artists' community in northern New Mexico. Her friends lent her an adobe art studio near a stream, beneath huge cottonwood trees. She loved the large north windows that overlooked a green meadow where black-and-white ponies grazed. Soon she became highly energized — laughing, excited, and spellbound — with the wonders and wideness of New Mexico.

Georgia liked to ride a horse into the foothills of the mountains to get a feel for the distances of the landscape she was painting and to watch the light fade. The rampant gray sage crept up against the base of violet mountains, reminding her of waves lapping against a seashore. She found fossils of shells in her "sea of sage."

During a pack trip with friends at the ranch of novelist D. H. Lawrence, Georgia lay on a long bench and looked up at a giant pine tree and the starry sky. She later painted her memory of it — *The Lawrence Tree* — by using a technique called foreshortening. She made the base of the tree trunk, which fills the upper left part of the canvas, look many times larger than it really was. The top of the trunk, at the center of the canvas, appears quite small. In the painting the distance between the base and the top of the trunk is much shorter than is the distance on a real tree trunk. In this way — through foreshortening — Georgia expressed the power she sensed about the tree.

Georgia O'Keeffe. **The Lawrence Tree.** *1929. Oil on canvas. 31$^1/_{16}$ × 39$^3/_{16}$ inches. Wadsworth Atheneum, Hartford. The Ella Gallup Sumner and Mary Catlin Sumner Collection.* When Georgia viewed D. H. Lawrence's giant pine tree from an unusual angle, she knew she wanted to capture the image on canvas.

Ranchos de Taos Church
(front view). *Author's photograph. 1990.*
The Ranchos de Taos Church looks today as it did hundreds of years ago when the early Spanish settlers built the mission by hand. Underneath the smooth layer of mud and straw, bricks made of adobe form the strong walls.

Ranchos de Taos Church
(rear view). *Author's photograph. 1990.*
For many years artists have been fascinated with the curved adobe forms on the rear side of the church. Georgia painted many versions of this side of the mission.

Like other artists in Taos, Georgia loved to walk behind the Ranchos de Taos Church, built by the early Spanish settlers, to study the structure's unusual adobe shapes and forms. At different times of the day, being observant of the changing light and sky, she painted her impressions of this church. For the next several years, she would paint many versions of the Ranchos de Taos Church.

Georgia gained strength and confidence from her first summer in New Mexico. She sensed that something in her life was ending as something else was beginning. Although she was not sure what it was, she was content to let it happen.

When it was time to return to New York, Georgia wondered what she could take with her to use as a model for painting. Because there were no flowers, she collected a barrel of bones to keep her working on paintings of the New Mexico country she had grown to love. She said it never occurred to her that bones have anything to do with death. Instead, she saw the bones — their line, shape, form, texture, and color — as being very lively subjects to paint.

Each year, when springtime came again, Georgia and Stieglitz were torn about whether she should spend yet another summer in New Mexico. Georgia's quiet determination to return always overcame Stieglitz's wishes for her to remain in New York.

Georgia O'Keeffe. **Ranchos Church — Taos.** *1930. Oil on canvas. 24 × 36 inches. Amon Carter Museum, Fort Worth (1971.16).*

Cow's Skull. *Author's photograph. 1990.*
On her long walks through the New Mexico desert, Georgia gathered bones much like this cow's skull to use as models for her paintings.

During other months, at Lake George, she pulled horses' and cows' skulls from her barrel of bones and painted images of them. In 1931 she created the oil painting *Cow's Skull: Red, White, and Blue.* As she worked she thought about the cattle drives she had watched thundering over the horizon near Amarillo, Texas. To Georgia, the cattle were a major part of the American experience. Yet to most of the New York artists, the inspiration for American art came from European thoughts and ideas. As Georgia painted along on her cow's skull on blue, she said to herself, "I'll make it an American painting." To make others notice, she placed red stripes down the sides. This work of art is considered a very personal American expression.

Stieglitz enjoyed exhibiting Georgia's Taos paintings at his new gallery, An American Place, near the Shelton. By now Georgia had become quite particular about her exhibits, and she often hung the paintings herself. She also had learned to prepare herself mentally for her exhibits. Before the show opened to the public, she always had her own private showing in which she made up her mind about each piece. Both flattery and criticism would "go down the same drain," leaving her unconcerned with others' opinions.

Stieglitz continued to exhibit and sell Georgia's drawings and paintings of the Southwest, where she spent summers for many years. However, he was twenty-three years older than O'Keeffe, and his health eventually began to fail. In 1946 Stieglitz died of a heart attack. Georgia missed her husband and partner very much.

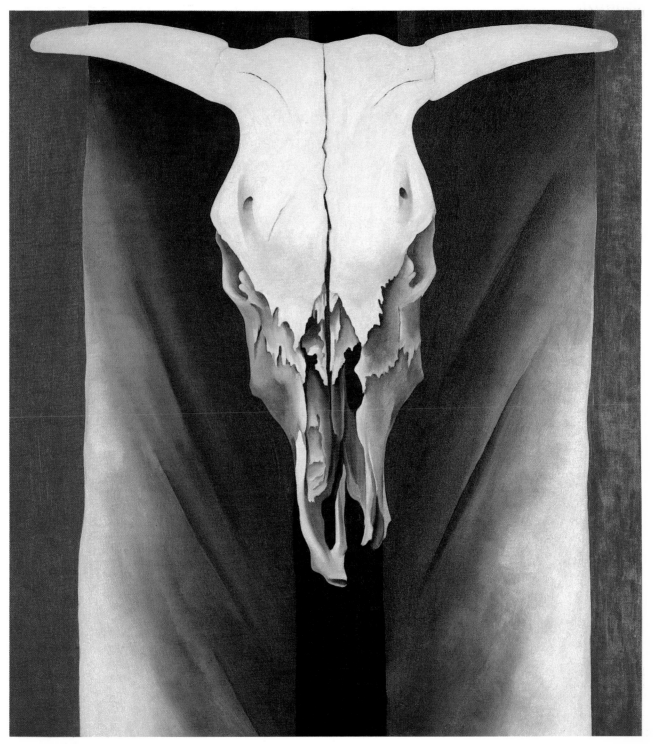

Georgia O'Keeffe. **Cow's
Skull: Red, White, and
Blue.** *1931. Oil on canvas.*
39⅞ × 35⅞ inches.
The Metropolitan Museum of
Art. The Alfred Stieglitz
Collection, 1952 (52.203).
Georgia O'Keeffe was very
much an American artist.
Through this painting she
paid tribute to her country.

For the rest of her long life Georgia made New Mexico her home. Although she traveled around the world, the artist treasured her privacy in New Mexico and was forever fascinated with the power of the mysterious desert landscape.

The desert bones continued to please her. Georgia said she was the sort of child who ate around the raisin on the cookie and around the hole in the doughnut, saving either the raisin or the edge of the hole for the last and best. So when she started painting the pelvis bones, she was interested in the holes in the bones — what she saw through them. Sometimes, as in *Pelvis with Moon,* she painted a landscape of her favorite mountain, the Pedernal, in the faraway distance. The bone appears to float very close to the viewer with nothing between the foreground and the background. Georgia explained that bones are most wonderful against the blue sky, which, as she said, "will always be there."

As she grew older, Georgia continued to create many wondrous works of art. In fact, by hanging enormous canvases on the walls of her garage, she painted a series of clouds — her largest works — after she had reached seventy-five. She continued to paint, sculpt, and travel for many more years.

Georgia O'Keeffe. **Pelvis with Moon.** *1943. Oil on canvas. 30 × 24 inches. Collection of the Norton Gallery of Art, West Palm Beach, Florida.*
When Georgia looked through the holes in pelvis bones, she saw the faraway sky. She took comfort in knowing that it would always be there.

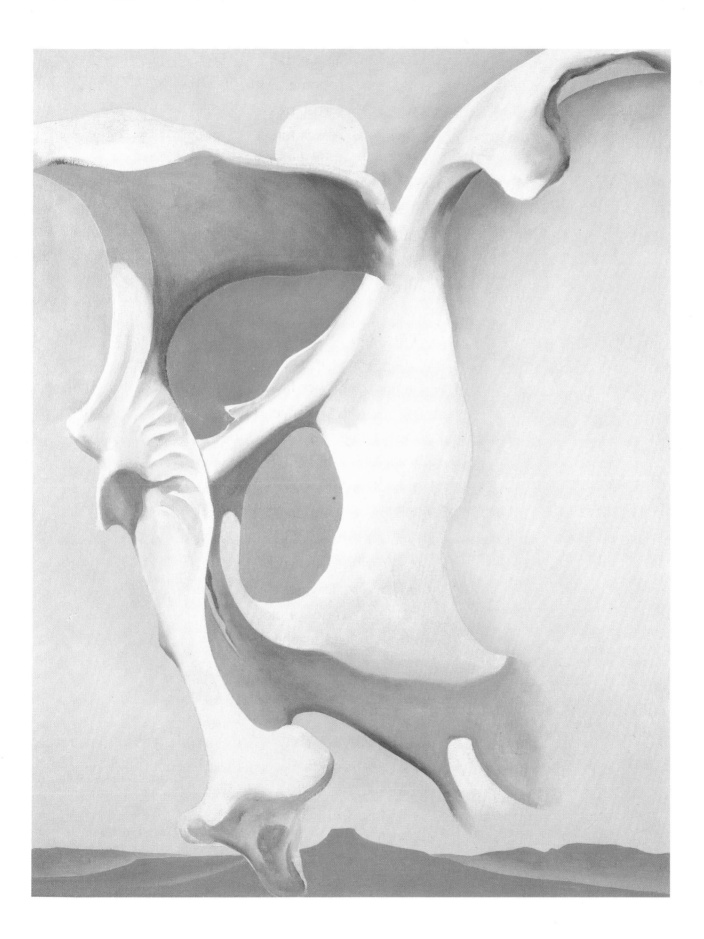

Laura Gilpin. **Georgia O'Keeffe.** *January 15, 1953.* © 1981 Laura Gilpin Collection, Amon Carter Museum, Fort Worth, Texas.

In 1986 Georgia O'Keeffe died peacefully in Santa Fe, New Mexico. During her legendary life of ninety-eight years she lived to see some of her nine hundred works of art exhibited in major art museums. Over the years she earned a fortune from her art. She received many awards, including the highest honor for a civilian — the United States Medal of Freedom. Although she rarely signed her artwork, Georgia left her mark on twentieth-century art in America and throughout the world.